# FORWARD

The Cross of Jesus is a familiar icon to most of the world, however few really know the depth of the  suffering that was experienced by Christ on that tree.  It was more than just the physical pain that He endured, but unfathomable tortures--even in the spirit realm. The depravity of sin can only be realized when one sees the extent to which the Father and Christ had to go to have that plague of the soul eradicated from the human · spirit.   Only a God of unconditional love would bother to redeem humanity from the miry pit into which we had fallen.   And only a Wonderful Savior who willingly became man would dare to become our ransom for sin.  Forever He will be praised,
 ***"Worthy! Worthy! Worthy is the Lamb that was slain!"***

# THE SUFFERINGS OF CHRIST

We truly do not know how much God loves us, nor the extent of the horrendous sufferings that Christ endured for us. If we knew even a small fraction of what He went through, we could never question His great love for each of us. He desires to bless us in spite of ourselves! His love is so deep--so expansive! It takes divine revelation from the Father to fully comprehend it!

> *"I bow my knees unto the Father of our Lord Jesus Christ ... that He would grant you [to] be able to comprehend with all saints what is the breadth, and length, and depth, and height; and to know the love of Christ, which passes knowledge ..."* (Ephesians 3:14, 18, 19)

To understand God's love, we must start at the beginning when He created man in His own image:

> *"And God said, Let Us make man in Our image, after Our likeness: and let them have dominion... So God created man in his own image, in the image of God created he him; male and female created he them. And God*

*blessed them, and God said unto them, Be fruitful, and multiply, and replenish the earth, and subdue it... And God said, Behold, I have given you every herb bearing seed, which is upon the face of all the earth, and every tree, in the which is the fruit of a tree yielding seed; to you it shall be for meat... And the Lord God planted a garden eastward in Eden; and there He put man whom He had formed ... and made every tree that is pleasant to see and good for food."* [1]

Here we see that man was not an after-thought to God, but that all of creation was made with mankind in mind. God is a wonderful, loving Father! I think of how my son and daughter-in-love are such loving, thoughtful parents. Every room of their home is filled with items for "little Henry" to give him comfort, protection, and enjoyment. Even so, God created man, and ensured every possible delight was given to him: He provided Adam with a perfect "help meet" (human companionship, a wife); made him a beautiful garden

---

[1] Genesis 1:26, 29; 2:8, 9

with nutritious, delicious food; and gave him a purpose in tending the garden. God even trusted Adam enough to give him a free will. Adam was not a robot who mechanically would obey God's every command. Adam was an independent entity from God the Father, with his own mind, will, thoughts, and emotions. In this way, the relationship between Adam and the Father would be a matter of Adam's will—his own choice. He could *choose* to reciprocate the love of his Heavenly Father.

As a doting father, God delighted seeing His children learn to subdue the earth that He had so masterfully created for them. He had a special time every day when He would meet with Adam and Eve--just to spend time fellowshipping with them![2] It was a beautiful relationship between the Creator and man, the crown of His creation. In the Bible's genealogy, Adam is actually called *"the son of God."*[3] All was well in paradise!

### *Has* God Said?

God had given one commandment to Adam, which was *not* to eat of the tree of the knowledge of good and evil.

---

[2] Genesis 3:8
[3] Luke 3:38

Of all the other thousands of trees in the garden he could partake freely, but that one tree was off-limits. If Adam ate of it, he would bring death upon himself. Loving parents will give their children perimeters. There are rules, and they are set in place for the child's good... for their safety and protection. So was God's law set for mankind's protection:

> *"the LORD God took the man and put him into the garden of Eden to dress it and to keep it. And the LORD God commanded the man, saying, Of every tree of the garden you may freely eat: But of the tree of the knowledge of good and evil, you shall not eat of it: for in the day that you eat of it, you shall surely die."[4]*

Adam and Eve enjoyed living in paradise ... a place of love, peace, and prosperity. And then, the unthinkable happened. Eve listened to the devil, who told her that God had lied to them, and she ate the forbidden fruit. Adam, however, was not fooled. He *knew* God's word was true, but decided to *ignore* the Father's warning!

---

[4] Genesis 2:15-17

*"And when the woman saw that the tree was good for food, and that it was pleasant to the eyes, and a tree to be desired to make one wise, she took of the fruit thereof, and did eat, and gave also unto her husband with her; AND HE DID EAT."*[5]

Eve was deceived; but not the man: *"And Adam was not deceived, but the woman being deceived was in the transgression."*[6] When offered the fruit, Adam willingly ate of it.

As happens so often, when God blesses His children with much, they take His love for granted. Adam decided he no longer needed to listen to God… after all, he was lord of his earthly domain in the garden. It is pride and presumption when we think that God's commands do not apply to us, and that we can blatantly disregard them and do as we please. That is what Adam did. Scripture tells us that Eve was deceived by the devil. She believed the serpent's lie that God was trying to withhold something good from her, and that nothing bad would happen if she

---

[5] Genesis 3:6
[6] I Timothy 2:14

ate of the tree.[7]  Adam knew exactly what he was doing. He *chose* to disobey.  He knew God's command, and that it was true, but disregarded it anyway!  How often do we flirt with sin-- lust, pride, anger, malice--and think, *"Oh, God understands... He knows I'm just flesh!"* And we never repent.  We continue stubbornly in our own way, rebelling against God's Word!  Lord, forgive us!

Why did Adam willfully transgress God's Law?  Had he put Eve above God?  Was he more concerned about pleasing his wife than obeying Almighty God?  How many relationships have we allowed to come before God's will in our lives?  Was it pride: *"No one can tell me what I can or cannot do"*?  Whatever his reason, Adam willfully broke covenant with His Heavenly Father, and he reaped the wages of his sin—eternal death and separation from God![8]

Did this take the Father by surprise?  Being the Omniscient God, no. But being a loving Father, it caused Him to weep--utterly broken-hearted.[9]  His son had just

---

[7] Genesis 3:1-7
[8] Romans 6:23
[9] Jeremiah 13:17

died … Man could no longer have fellowship with the Creator, nor God with man. Man's sin had separated him from God.

## The Master Plan

But all was not lost! From the ions of time before time, God knew what would happen to the crown of His creation. Though God would not breach man's free-will and stop him from sinning, He could offer an antidote for the sickness of his soul. In the High Court of Heaven, man was guilty as charged. But the Judge of all Judges could choose to pardon His lost son. And yet, being a just Judge, it would not be fair to let a transgressor go free, son or not! Sin had to be paid for, for it is utterly wicked and contrary to the nature of God and His Kingdom. The darkness of sin cannot exist in the Kingdom of Light! How could God be *merciful* in pardoning His son, and yet *just*, and not allow the sin to go unpunished? Man had to pay the price for his rebellion. The verdict was: GUILTY! The sentence: DEATH! *"The wages of sin is death"*.[10] The sinner

---

[10]Romans 6:23

12

(man) must die. But perhaps God could find a substitute to die in Adam's place!

## The Just for the Unjust

I recently met a man whose father is an elderly pastor in South Georgia. He shared an experience he had growing up that left a profound impression in his heart and mind. As typical boys, he and his younger brother had their share of fights and mischievous antics. Occasionally, their behavior warranted a spanking. When he and his brother were especially bad his mother would give them the foreboding warning, *"Just wait until your father gets home!"* When their father got home, he would give them their spanking, but only *after* he would lovingly explain from the Bible why he must discipline them. Knowing that they had disappointed their beloved father hurt them just as much as the spanking, if not more!

On one such day, the pastor brought the boys to the back room for the customary discussion of their behavior prior to the spanking. But that day the father said, "Today we are going to do something different." The two boys looked apprehensively at each other, wondering if their spanking was going to be much worse. The regular spankings were usually enough deterrent to keep them straight for at least a little while!

The father took off his belt, handed it to the older son, and said, "Today I'm going to take your punishment. I want you to spank me." The son was shocked, and then dismayed. He thought, "How can I spank my loving father for what *I did wrong*!" At the father's insistence, he finally did "spank" his father (barely tapping him with the belt). The younger son also could not bring himself to punish his father, and also barely tapped him. As this grown son relayed the story, I could see in his eyes that this lesson of love was forever imbedded in his soul... a graphic demonstration of how God extended mercy to us when we deserved punishment, and allowed an Innocent Substitute to take our place. The just for the unjust ...

So, the Heavenly Father wanted to extend mercy to Adam. He searched all of creation for a worthy substitute to take man's punishment. He decided to allow for innocent animal blood to be shed for man's sin, but that would only be a temporary covering. Since man sinned, it would ultimately require that human blood be shed to fully pay for Adam's transgression. It is only through blood that sin can be forgiven.[11] But in order for the blood to atone for sin, it would have to be *innocent, pure* human blood. Where could God find sinless blood to pay for Adam's transgression? Scripture tells us that ***"all have sinned and come short of the glory of God"*** and ***"there is none righteous, no not one!"***[12] There *was no* innocent human blood to be found! Mankind was doomed to a state of eternal punishment and death— complete separation from their Heavenly Father.

## From Heaven's Balconies

Then, from the balconies of Heaven a voice was heard!

> ***"Sacrifice and offerings You did not desire, but a body You have prepared for Me: In [animal] burnt offerings and sacrifices for sin You had no pleasure. Then said I, Look! I come to do Thy will, O God."***[13]

---

[11] Leviticus 17:11
[12] Romans 3:23
[13] Hebrews 10:6, 7

The perfect Son of God, second Person of the Godhead, stepped up to be the sacrificial substitute. He offered to come as man, in a flesh and blood human body, so that the penalty of death could be paid by innocent blood. Jesus was the *"Lamb of God who came to take away the sin of the world."*[14] Mankind had been sold under sin. It would take His precious, undefiled Blood to wash away the sin of mankind. That Blood would be the atoning sacrifice needed to ransom our souls from sin and death!

So, in the fulness of time, God sent His Son, born of a virgin, to live a perfect human life in the flesh[15]. He was called, "Immanuel—God with us." He would become our substitute sin-bearer. It was incredible humbling for the Son of God to partake of a human body—to be fully God and yet fully man! Jesus' body was totally human, complete with pain sensors, nerves, muscles, tendons, and blood vessels--just like any other man. And the death that He would have to die for mankind would be a most horrific, painful death: that of the torturous crucifixion. WHY would He do it? *Why?* Because, *"the*

---

[14] John 1:29
[15] Isaiah 7:14

*Son of God loved [us] and gave Himself for us, to wash us from our sins in His Own Blood."[16]*

And why would the Heavenly Father allow for His Beloved, Holy Son to become our ransom? *"God so loved the world that He gave His only Begotten Son, that whosoever would believe in Him should not perish, but have ever lasting life."[17]*

If you had a beloved only child--innocent and loving-- would you allow him to be tortured and killed for a world full of hateful, murderous, ungrateful, violent, vile, perverted sinners? Wouldn't you say, *"Let them die for their own sin!"* And yet, God the Father's love for lost humanity was so intense... so unconditional, that He was willing to love the unlovely. He knew mankind was in the grip of satan's delusion and bondage of sin, and that we were all destined for eternal, hellish punishment unless He intervened. And intervened He did! He sent us Heaven's Best!

---

[16] Galatians 2:20; Revelation 1:5
[17] John 3:16

## Just-If-I'd Never Sinned!

God is just and the justifier of them that believe in Jesus. He is *just*, in that He will not allow sin to go unpunished. We would consider a judge who would let criminals go free a crooked judge! So, God could not let sinful man off without their sin being paid for. God is also the *justifier*—making us just and righteous in His sight as He looks at us through Jesus' shed Blood. It is *just as if we had never sinned* after the cleansing Blood of Jesus is applied to our hearts! It has the power to cleanse us from ALL unrighteousness! Thank God! What a wonderful Savior. What a merciful and forgiving God!

## He Bore It All

There were so many levels of suffering and pain that Jesus endured for us--emotional, physical, and even spiritual punishment and abuse. Anything that you may have endured in your life that caused terrible pain and grief--multiply that by billions! *That* is what Christ experienced on our behalf. He was the sacrificial Lamb, the scapegoat, upon Whom the sins of the whole world were laid.

## Rejected By Men

Isaiah 53 tells us that Jesus was *"despised and rejected of men..."* And that He was! It broke Christ's heart to be so hated and rejected by the very ones for whom He came to die. The God of the universe in the form of man was looked down upon with great contempt by mortal man. He was, in their estimation, of no account. He was *"despised of the people."* All that passed by the cross laughed and mocked Jesus saying, *"He trusted in the LORD... let Him deliver Jesus if He really delights in him!"* The very thoughts of Jesus' heart were prophesied, telling the great shame and hurt that He felt:

*"You have known my reproach, and my shame, and my dishonor: mine adversaries are all before you. Reproach has broken my heart; and I am full of heaviness: and I looked for some to take pity, but there was none; and for comforters, but I found none. They gave me also gall for my meat; and in my thirst they gave me vinegar to drink... they persecute him whom you*

*have smitten; and they talk to the grief of those whom you have wounded."[18]*

If you have no regard for someone… if they mean *nothing* to you, it doesn't bother you if they do not like you or if they reject you. You couldn't care less! What does *their* opinion matter! But, if you have great love and care for someone, their rejection hurts you to the heart. *They can* break your heart by rejecting you. Jesus' great care and love for us made Him vulnerable. He was so deeply hurt by the venomous hatred spewed out of the people, that it literally broke His heart.

The elite, as well as the "scum of society," derided Jesus as He hung in excruciating pain. The drunkards laughed and mocked Jesus in song as they meandered by His cross—all the while His blood dripped down for them:

*"They that sit in the gate speak against me; and I was the song of the drunkards. Deliver me out of the mire, and let me not sink: let me be*

---

18 Psalm 69

*delivered from them that hate me... let not the pit shut her mouth upon me..."[19]*

## Rejected By His Neighbors

Jesus was reproached by those of His own community:

*"I was a reproach among all mine enemies, but especially among my neighbors, and a fear to mine acquaintance: they that did see me without fled from me. I am forgotten as a dead man out of mind: I am like a broken vessel. For I have heard the slander of many: fear was on every side: while they took counsel together against me, they devised to take away my life. My heart is sore pained within me..."[20]*

## Rejected By Friends

Those with whom Jesus had close fellowship also turned on Him. No one cared for His soul:

*"My heart pants, my strength fails me: as for the light of mine eyes, it also is gone from me. My lovers and my friends stand aloof from*

---

[19] Psalm 69:15
[20] Psalm 31:11

*my sore; and my kinsmen stand afar off. They also that seek after my life lay snares for me: and they that seek my hurt speak mischievous things, and imagine deceits all the day long...Mine enemies speak evil of me, When shall he die, and his name perish?"[21]*

*"...Yes, my own familiar friend, in whom I trusted, which did eat of my bread, has lifted up his heel against me. As with a sword in my bones, mine enemies reproach me; while they say daily unto me, Where is your God? ...Because of the voice of the enemy, because of the oppression of the wicked: for they cast iniquity upon me, and in wrath they hate me."[22]*

## Rejected By Family

Even Jesus' family rejected Him. Psalm 69 describes the shame that Jesus felt when His own brothers disowned Him--acting as if they did not even know Him:

---

[21] Psalm 38:10
[22] Psalm 41:9

22

*"I am weary of my crying: my throat is dried: mine eyes fail while I wait for my God. They that hate me without a cause are more than the hairs of mine head: they that would destroy me, being mine enemies wrongfully, are mighty... Because for your sake I have borne reproach; shame has covered my face. I am become a stranger unto MY BRETHREN, and an alien unto MY MOTHER'S CHILDREN..."*

Jesus' half-brothers and half-sisters (children of Joseph and Mary's union after Jesus was born) hated Him. The townspeople assumed that Jesus was Joseph's son and treated Him as just "the carpenter." He had no honor in His hometown, and certainly not among His family!

Can you imagine being a sibling to Jesus? He was a perfect son. He never sinned. He was fully obedient and always manifested the fruit of the Spirit! It would have been natural for Joseph and Mary to compare the siblings to Him: "Why can't you be more like Jesus?" was likely said more than once in their household. His brothers resented Him. They accused Jesus of being crazy when

He began His preaching ministry.[23] They even tried to put Jesus in harm's way by encouraging Him to go to Jerusalem when they knew the Jews there wanted Him dead![24]  Job prophesied that Jesus' friends and family would turn against Him and mock Him:

*"He has put my brethren far from me, and my acquaintance truly are estranged from me. My kinsfolk have failed, and my familiar friends have forgotten me... All my close friends abhorred me: and they whom I loved are turned against me. And now am I their song, yea, I am their byword. They abhor me, they flee far from me, and spare not to spit in my face. My friends scorn me..."*

## Rejected By God

Even more painful than the cross was the anguish that Jesus experienced by being rejected by His Heavenly Father.  Consider Jesus' cry from the cross as He pleads with God to acknowledge Him:

---

[23] Mark 3:21,31 (Note: the term "friends" is not an accurate translation here. In the Greek it is actually, "ones He belonged to" (i.e., His family))
[24] John 7:1-5

*"My God, my God, why have you forsaken me? why are you so far from helping me, and from the words of my roaring? O my God, I cry in the daytime, but you hear not; and in the night season, and am not silent..."*[25]

The Father refused to look upon Jesus as He suffered on the tree. Scripture tells us that from twelve noon until 3:00 p.m. the sun was darkened. It was then that the Father would execute His righteous judgment upon sin:

*"Shall not the land tremble for this, and everyone mourn that dwells therein? ... And it shall come to pass in that day, says the Lord GOD, that I will cause the sun to go down at noon, and I will darken the earth in the clear day: And I will turn your feasts into mourning, and all your songs into lamentation; and I will bring up sackcloth upon all loins, and baldness upon every head; and I will make it as the*

---

[25] Psalm 22

*mourning of an Only Son, and the end thereof as a bitter day.*"[26]

It was a bitter day when the Father placed upon Jesus the iniquity of us all, making Him the final Sacrifice for sin. The scripture states that God cannot look upon sin: *"Thou art of purer eyes than to behold evil and cannot not look on iniquity ..."*[27] Because God cannot look upon sin, the Father veiled His eyes from beholding His Beloved Son with thick clouds! He had to turn His back on Jesus. For the first time in eternity, communion between The Son and His Father was severed. In utter despair and astonishment, Jesus cried out to God, *"WHY have You forsaken Me?"* and realized that the Father no longer heard His prayers. He was completely alone; completely forsaken ...

## Surely He Bore our Pain

The utter rejection from all those that Jesus loved crushed His heart. But compounding the emotional pain was the torturous, physical pain of the crucifixion itself. The Gospel accounts are very "non-descript" about the Cross

---

[26] Amos 8:8-10, Matthew 27:45
[27] Habakkuk 1:13

of Christ.    They simply say, "And they crucified Him..."[28]    The writers give little detail about what actually happened to Jesus' body on the Cross, but medical science, history and archeology have much to say about crucifixion.

Though Jesus was God, He endured the physical agony of the cross as a flesh and blood Man. He felt all the pain as they beat Him with a cat-o'-nine-tails (Roman scourging whip) that left long rows of ripped flesh on His back, so deep that his entrails were exposed. He *felt* it as they beat and pummeled His face so that it was beyond recognition:

> *"Many a time have they afflicted me from my youth: yet they have not prevailed against me. The plowers plowed upon my back: they made long their furrows... As many were astonished at you; his visage was so marred more than any man, and his form more than the sons of men: So shall he sprinkle many nations"*[29]

---

[28] Matthew 27:35
[29] Psalm 129:3; Isaiah 52:14

Following the scourging (which was so severe that it often brought the victims to the brink of death) was the actual crucifixion. Crucifixion was a favorite form of capital punishment in the Roman world, as it not only inflicted excruciating pain on the criminal for extended periods of time, but also demonstrated publicly the authority of Rome. If some wanted to disregard Roman Law and commit a crime, they could expect a similar fate. It was a great deterrent against a Jewish rebellion when people saw criminals hanging in agony (sometimes for days) in conspicuous public places. It was a graphic warning that they should not test the Roman authority.

## Jesus' Execution

Already weak and near shock from the pain and loss of blood from the scourging, Jesus carried the cross beam of His cross several hundred yards to the hill of crucifixion, Golgotha. It was there that the Roman soldiers pounded half inch spikes into each wrist and His feet to support His body on the cross. He felt every bit of the pain as the spikes sent searing pain through His arms, and legs, and as His bones were pulled out of joint as He hung on the cross. David graphically prophesied of the crucifixion, alluding to the Roman soldiers that surrounded Jesus (described as "dogs," since they were frequently homosexuals), and of the demonic hoards ("bulls of Bashan" and "roaring lion") that encompassed Him as He suffered:

*"Be not far from me; for trouble is near; for there is none to help. Many bulls have compassed me: strong bulls of Bashan have beset me round. They gaped upon me with their mouths, as a ravening and a roaring lion. I am poured out like water, and all my bones are out of joint: my heart is like wax; it is melted in the midst of my bowels. My strength is dried up like a potsherd; and my tongue cleaves to my jaws; and Thou hast brought me into the dust of death. For dogs have compassed me: the assembly of the wicked have enclosed me: they pierced my hands and my feet. I may tell all my bones: they look and stare upon me. They part my garments among them, and cast lots upon my vesture..."*

Medical doctor, C. Truman Davis, describes the physical trauma to the body in crucifixion in this manner:

*"As the victim slowly sags down with more weight on the nails in the wrists, excruciating pain shoots along the fingers and up the arms to explode in the brain — the nails in the wrists are putting pressure on the median nerves. As He pushes Himself upward to avoid this stretching torment, He places His full weight on the nail through His feet. Again there is the searing agony of the nail tearing through the nerves between the metatarsal bones of the feet. At this point, as the arms fatigue, great waves of cramps sweep over the muscles, knotting them in deep, relentless, throbbing pain. With these cramps comes the inability to push Himself upward. Hanging by his arms, the pectoral muscles are paralyzed and the intercostal muscles are unable to act. Air can be drawn into the lungs, but cannot be exhaled.*

*Jesus fights to raise Himself in order to get even one short breath."[30]*

Then Dr. Davis goes on to explain that the final facet of the torture brings horrendous pain to the chest as the heart becomes compressed as serum fills the sac around the heart. Due to dehydration and loss of tissue fluid, the blood thickens. The heart can barely pump the thickened blood and so oxygen is no longer adequately delivered to the body. As David prophesied, Jesus' heart was like wax... melting in the midst of Him. Unlike most crucifixion victims who die of suffocation (not able to get air into the lungs), Jesus died of a broken heart.

## Forgiveness Through Jesus' Sacrifice

Isaiah prophesied the "suffering Servant's" afflictions hundreds of years before Christ fulfilled it on the Cross. It was God's eternal plan to redeem man back to God through Jesus' sacrifice:

*"...to whom is the arm of the LORD revealed? ...He is despised and rejected of men; a man of sorrows, and acquainted with grief: and we hid*

---

[30] http://www1.cbn.com/medical-view-of-the-crucifixion-of-jesus-christ

*as it were our faces from him; he was despised, and we esteemed him not. Surely he has borne our griefs, and carried our sorrows: yet we did esteem him stricken, smitten of God, and afflicted. But he was wounded for our transgressions, he was bruised for our iniquities: the chastisement of our peace was upon him; and with his stripes we are healed. All we like sheep have gone astray; we have turned everyone to his own way; and the LORD has laid on him the iniquity of us all"[31]*

The Spotless Lamb of God fulfilled all of the ancient prophecies that predicted His suffering on the cross, even speaking the Psalms verbatim as He hung on the tree:

*"Now from the sixth hour there was darkness over all the land unto the ninth hour. And about the ninth hour Jesus cried with a loud voice, saying, 'Eli, Eli, lama sabachthani?' that is to say, 'My God, my God, why have You forsaken me?' Some of them that stood there, when they*

---

[31] Isaiah 53

*heard that, said, This man calls for Elias. Jesus, cried again with a loud voice, 'IT IS FINISHED.' He then bowed His head, saying, 'Father, into thy hands I commend My spirit': and having said thus, He gave up the ghost. And, behold, the veil of the temple was torn in two from the top to the bottom; and the earth did quake, and the rocks split; Now when the centurion, and they that were with him, watching Jesus, saw the earthquake, and those things that were done, they feared greatly, saying, 'Truly this was the Son of God.'"[32]*

When Jesus cried out, *"It is finished!"* He was heralding the fact that the final Sacrifice for sin had been offered. The perfect atonement had been provided by a sinless, innocent Man, who allowed His Blood to be shed to atone for transgressions of Adam and of all mankind. The price was PAID IN FULL! God's justice had been completely satisfied through the death of His own Son! Now God could extend mercy to us, for the Precious

---

[32] Matthew 27, Luke 23, John 19

Blood could cleanse us from sin. Thank God! We can be forgiven simply by believing what Jesus did for us!

*"... for he was cut off out of the land of the living: for the transgression of my people was he stricken. And he made his grave with the wicked, and with the rich in his death; because he had done no violence, neither was any deceit in his mouth. Yet it pleased the LORD to bruise him; he has put him to grief: when you shalt MAKE HIS SOUL AN OFFERING FOR SIN... He shall see of the travail of his soul, and shall be satisfied: by his knowledge shall my righteous servant justify many; for he shall bear their iniquities."[33]*

Jesus died an innocent man on the cross of dishonor and shame. Today if one visits the "Place of the Skull" (the hill of crucifixion outside of Old Jerusalem), it is still a place of disregard and desecration. A bus station on a busy street is at the base of it, with garbage strewn around. Jesus was crucified outside of the city gates

---

[33] Isaiah 53:10, 11

where the main thoroughfares met. There Jesus hung, humiliated and suffering unspeakable pain. He did not have to--but He chose to.

## No Greater Love

While Jesus was on the cross, there was yet another realm of suffering that He had to endure. It was so dreadful, that it makes the torture of the crucifixion pale by comparison. It was the suffering that Jesus endured by taking the *punishment* for our sin. Truly, it is only Jesus' Blood that can remit and cleanse us from sin. For, *"without the shedding of blood, there is no remission."*[34] But sin also has penalties--consequences and repercussions--that must be faced as a result of sin. In other words, though our sin can be forgiven, the consequences of sin can cause one to have to suffer.

For example, a man can lead a life of debauchery and sin and end up in jail with terrible diseases in his body. God will graciously forgive that man if he comes to Christ in true repentance and gives his life to the Lord. However,

---

[34] Hebrews 9:22

the *consequences* of his sin *may not* be taken away. He may die in prison with AIDS in great pain, and yet still be forgiven. The sin of his soul was taken care of. However, the punishment of his sin was not removed.

Our sin warrants great punishment to be meted out to us. Jesus not only paid the price to cover and forgive our sin, but He also took the *punishment* that our sin deserves. His shed Blood forgives and cleanses us from sin. But Jesus also suffered and paid for the *consequences* of sin.

## In the Heart of the Earth

In the spirit realm when Jesus gave up the Ghost, He instantly descended into the heart of the earth. ***"As Jonah was three days and three nights in the whale's belly; so shall the Son of man be three days and three nights the heart of the earth."***[35] There, in the "heart of the earth" (hell), He actually endured God's wrath for us. The Greek term for hell is "Gehenna," a place of everlasting punishment. The Hebrew word for hell is *"Sheol."* Though Sheol is generally considered to be the resting place of the dead, there were two compartments to hell

---

[35] Matthew 12:40

before the Cross and resurrection of Christ.[36]   One was for the righteous, and the other for the wicked.   The wicked were punished and tormented in flames, and on the other side of a great chasm, the righteous were comforted in "Abraham's bosom."   Peter preached that Jesus experienced the *"pains of death in hell"* for us, as prophesied in Psalm 16:

*"Ye men of Israel, hear these words; Jesus of Nazareth, a man approved of God among you by miracles and wonders and signs, which God did by him in the midst of you, as ye yourselves also know: Him, being delivered by the determinate counsel and foreknowledge of God, ye have taken, and by wicked hands have crucified and slain: Whom God hath raised up, having loosed the PAINS OF DEATH: because it was not possible that he should be holden of it. For David speaketh concerning him, I foresaw the Lord always before my face, for he is on my right hand, that I should not be moved: Therefore did my heart rejoice, and my*

---

[36]Luke 16:22-26

tongue was glad; moreover also my flesh shall rest in hope: Because thou wilt not LEAVE MY SOUL IN HELL, neither wilt thou suffer thine Holy One to see corruption. Thou hast made known to me the ways of life; thou shalt make me full of joy with thy countenance. Men and brethren, let me freely speak unto you of the patriarch David, that he is both dead and buried, and his sepulcher is with us unto this day. Therefore being a prophet, and knowing that God had sworn with an oath to him, that of the fruit of his loins, according to the flesh, he would raise up Christ to sit on his throne; He seeing this before spake of the resurrection of Christ, that HIS SOUL WAS NOT LEFT IN HELL, neither his flesh did see corruption. This Jesus hath God raised up, whereof we all are witnesses. Therefore being by the right hand of God exalted, and having received of the Father the promise of the Holy Ghost, he hath shed forth this, which ye now see and hear. For David is not ascended into the heavens: but he *saith himself, The LORD said unto my Lord, Sit thou on my right hand, Until I make thy foes thy footstool. Therefore let all the house of Israel know assuredly, that God hath made that same Jesus, whom ye have crucified, both Lord and Christ. "[37]*

Psalm 18 also prophesied that Messiah Jesus would experience the *"sorrows"* (pains) of hell, but would be raised up to reign over the heathen:

*"The SORROWS OF DEATH COMPASSED ME, and the floods of ungodly men made me afraid. The SORROWS OF HELL compassed me about: the SNARES OF DEATH PREVENTED me. In my distress I called upon the LORD, and cried unto my God: he heard my voice out of his temple, and my cry came before him, even into his ears. <u>Then the earth shook and trembled; the foundations also of the hills moved and were shaken</u>, because he was wroth... He sent from above, he took me, he*

---

[37] Acts 2:23-27

*drew me out of many waters... Thou hast delivered me from the strivings of the people; and THOU HAST MADE ME THE HEAD OF THE HEATHEN: a people whom I have not known shall serve me."*[38]

I believe that this Psalm references the earthquake that occurred when Jesus gave up the Ghost on the Cross.[39] In the spirit realm, there is no time. In an instant when Jesus descended into hell, He experienced the full punishment and pain of death and hell, (and even the *wrath* of Almighty God!) His suffering was so intense, so horrendous, that it completely satisfied the punishment that our sin deserved. Acts 2 and Hebrews 2 reference the prophecies of Psalms 16, 18 and 116, saying Christ fulfilled these when He suffered the *"pains of death and hell."*

### Thy Fierce Wrath

Two of the most terrifying descriptions of Jesus enduring punishment for us are found in Psalms 88 and 89. They

---

[38] Psalm 18:4-7, 43
[39] Matthew 27:51

speak of God's wrath being poured out upon His "Anointed":

*"For my soul is full of troubles: and my life draws nigh unto the grave. I am counted with them that go down into the pit: I am as a man that hath no strength: FREE AMONG THE DEAD, LIKE THE SLAIN THAT LIE IN THE GRAVE, whom You remember no more: and they are cut off from thy hand. Thou has laid me in the LOWEST PIT, in darkness, in the deeps. THY WRATH LIES HARD UPON ME, and Thou has afflicted me with all thy waves. Selah. Thou hast put away mine acquaintance far from me; Thou hast made me an abomination unto them: I am shut up, and I cannot come forth. Mine eye mourns by reason of affliction: LORD, I have called daily upon Thee, I have stretched out my hands unto thee. WILT THOU SHEW WONDERS TO THE DEAD? shall the dead arise and praise thee? Selah. Shall Thy lovingkindness be declared IN*

*THE GRAVE? or Thy faithfulness in destruction? Shall Thy wonders be known in the dark? and Thy righteousness in the land of forgetfulness? But unto Thee have I cried, O LORD; and in the morning shall my prayer prevent thee. LORD, why do You cast off my soul? why do You hide Your face from me? I am afflicted and ready to die from my youth up: WHILE I SUFFER THY TERRORS I AM DISTRACTED. THY FIERCE WRATH GOETH OVER ME; THY TERRORS HAVE CUT ME OFF.*[40]*"*

*"I have made a covenant with my chosen, I have sworn unto David my servant, THY SEED* [Messiah] *WILL I ESTABLISH FOREVER, and build up thy throne to all generations. Selah. ... He shall cry unto me, Thou art my father, my God, and the rock of my salvation. Also I will make him MY FIRSTBORN, higher than the kings of the*

---

[40] Psalm 88

*earth. My mercy will I keep for him for evermore, and my covenant shall stand fast with him. His seed also will I make to endure for ever, and his throne as the days of heaven...*

*Once have I sworn by my holiness that I will not lie unto David. His seed shall endure for ever, and his throne as the sun before me. It shall be established for ever as the moon, and as a faithful witness in heaven. Selah. But thou hast cast off and abhorred, THOU HAST BEEN WROTH WITH THINE ANOINTED. Thou hast made void the covenant of thy servant: thou hast profaned his crown by casting it to the ground. Thou hast broken down all his hedges; thou hast brought his strong holds to ruin. All that pass by the way spoil him: he is a reproach to his neighbours. Thou hast set up the right hand of his adversaries; thou hast made all his enemies to rejoice. Thou hast also turned the edge of his sword, and hast not made him to stand in the battle. Thou hast made his glory to cease, and cast his throne down to the ground. The days of his youth hast thou shortened: thou hast covered him with shame. Selah. HOW LONG, LORD? WILT THOU HIDE THYSELF FOR EVER? SHALL THY WRATH BURN LIKE FIRE? Remember how short my time is: wherefore hast thou made all men in vain? What man is he that liveth, and shall not see death? SHALL HE DELIVER HIS SOUL FROM THE HAND OF THE GRAVE? Selah. Lord, where are thy former lovingkindnesses, which thou swarest unto David in thy truth? Remember, Lord, the reproach of thy servants; how I do bear in my bosom the reproach of all the mighty people; Wherewith thine enemies have reproached, O LORD; WHEREWITH THEY HAVE REPROACHED THE FOOTSTEPS OF THINE ANOINTED."[41]*

It is incredible! The Messiah, the King of Kings and LORD of Lords, endured the full brunt of God's wrath

---

[41] Psalm 89

44

for us! His suffering was so horrific... He took the punishment that all depraved humanity from time and eternity had due to them! Oh my! What a Savior!!

### The Victory March!

After Jesus endured that wrath, the Father was satisfied. Both sin and its eternal consequences had been paid for in full. Then He shook the earth from its foundations and delivered Jesus from the pains of death. Jesus then pursued His enemy, the devil, and wounded him so that he was not able to rise again! According to Psalm 18, it was then that God gave Jesus the necks of His enemies and made Jesus the *"head of the heathen."* Truly, Jesus took the keys of death, hell and the grave from satan, making a public spectacle of him, triumphing and defeating him through the Cross![42] Through Jesus' death,

> *"He destroyed him that had the power of death, that is, the devil; and delivered them who through fear of death were all their lifetime subject to bondage."[43]*

---

[42] Colossians 2:15; Revelation 1:18
[43] Hebrews 2:14, 15

## Preached in Hell!

For three days Jesus preached to the spirits of just men made perfect, whose souls were waiting in Abraham's bosom.[44] The repentant thief on the cross was there hearing the Gospel, for just a few hours before Jesus had promised, *"Today you will be with Me in paradise!"*[45]

After three days of proclaiming victory over death and hell, Jesus rose bodily from the grave and appeared for forty days to his disciples (even to 500 at one time!) They touched Jesus' nail scarred hands and ate with Him! It changed their lives forever. They were so convinced that Jesus Christ is the Son of God that they went into all the world preaching the Gospel, willing to lay down their lives to attest to the fact that "He is risen indeed!"

## You Can Know!

You too can have the assurance of eternal life through Jesus Christ if you will repent from your sins and follow Him as Lord of your life. *"If you will confess with your*

---

[44] I Peter 3:18, 19
[45] Luke 23:43

*mouth the LORD Jesus and believe in your heart that God raised Him from the dead, you shall be saved."*[46]
For God did not send His Son into the world to condemn the world, but that through Him, we might be saved!

Whom the Son sets free is free indeed! Thank God for the Cross! Thank God that Jesus was willing to pay in full the price for our redemption by His Precious Blood! What unsearchable love the Father has bestowed upon us, that we now can be called the *"sons of God"*![47] As His children, we will again enjoy God's fellowship in the heavenly Paradise forever! Amen!

---

[46] Romans 10:9, 10
[47] I John 3:1
NOTE: All Scripture references are from the King James Version.

Made in the USA
Middletown, DE
15 February 2022

61147813R00031